MW01171041

US ERROR COINS GUIDE 2025

A Collector's Guide to Identifying and Valuing Minting Mistakes

Merle Wallace

US ERROR COINS GUIDE 2025

Copyright Page

US ERROR COINS GUIDE 2025 by Merle Wallace

Copyright © 2025 by **Merle Wallace**

All rights reserved.

No part of this book may be reproduced, distributed, or transmitted in any form or by any means, including photocopying, recording, or other electronic or mechanical methods, without the prior written permission of the publisher, except in the case of brief quotations embodied in critical reviews and certain other noncommercial uses permitted by copyright law.

Disclaimer

This book is a work of nonfiction. The views expressed in this book are those of the author and do not necessarily reflect the views of the publisher. Every effort has been made to ensure the accuracy of the information presented. However, the author and publisher cannot be held responsible for any errors or omissions.

Table of Contents

INTRODUCTION

Overview of US Error Coins

U S error coins are a fascinating subset of numismatics, representing rare and unique flaws that occur during the minting process. These coins are not only interesting for their historical and technical significance, but also hold considerable value in the collector's market. An error coin occurs when a mistake happens at any stage of production—whether in the design, striking, or finishing process—that results in a coin that deviates from its intended appearance. These deviations can range from minor misalignments to dramatic, easily identifiable mistakes that make a coin one-of-a-kind.

Importance and Significance of Error Coins in Numismatics

In the world of coin collecting, error coins occupy a special place. They provide a glimpse into the intricate and sometimes imperfect process of coin production. For collectors, error coins are highly sought after for their rarity and their stories. A single coin with an error can tell a tale of how it was made, how it went unnoticed by mint workers, or how it was lost or hidden for decades. The value of error coins lies not only in their rarity but also in their historical context. Some error coins are prized for their rarity or the circumstances surrounding their production, making them invaluable treasures in a collector's portfolio.

In addition to their appeal to individual collectors, error coins have also become the focus of significant research and scholarship within the numismatic community. These coins help to identify flaws in the minting process and have even led to improvements in coin production methods over time.

Brief History of Error Coins in US Minting Processes

Error coins have been produced since the earliest days of the United States Mint. From the first coins struck in the late 18th century to the modern coinage of today, the US Mint has seen its fair share of errors.

Early US coins, such as the 1792 half dismes, were struck using hand-operated presses, which left ample room for mistakes. These early errors are some of the most valuable and highly prized by collectors today.

The industrialization of coin production, starting in the 19th century, brought with it increased efficiency and the introduction of more complex machinery. However, with the rise of automation came an increase in new types of errors—ranging from doubled dies and off-center strikes to more extreme defects like the famous 1943 copper penny. Despite advances in technology, human oversight and mechanical imperfections still lead to the occasional mistake, keeping error coins an ever-present and cherished aspect of numismatics.

In the 20th and 21st centuries, the Mint has implemented several measures to reduce errors, including better quality control and more advanced equipment. Yet, error coins still occasionally slip through the cracks, making them both rare and valuable for collectors. These coins are not just curiosities; they offer a deeper look into the evolving technology of the US Mint and the human element behind coin production.

CHAPTER ONE

What Are Error Coins?

Explanation of What Qualifies as an Error Coin

An error coin is a coin that has been produced with a flaw or mistake during the minting process, resulting in an irregularity from the intended design or striking. These errors can happen at various stages of production, including the design phase, planchet preparation, or even the actual coin striking. A coin must have a visible anomaly that was unintended during the minting process to be classified as an error. Some errors are very subtle and may go unnoticed by the public, while others are so glaring that they are immediately apparent.

What distinguishes an error coin from a regular coin is that the flaw or anomaly is typically not reproducible under normal production conditions. The rarity and uniqueness of an error coin make it highly collectible, and in some cases, quite valuable. It is important to note that errors should not be confused with damaged or altered coins; an error occurs during production, while damage can happen after the coin has left the mint.

Types of Errors

Error coins can be categorized into three main types: die errors, planchet errors, and striking errors. Each of these occurs at different stages of the minting process and results in a variety of visible flaws on the coin.

Die Errors:
These occur when the dies used to strike the coin (the tools that emboss the coin's design) develop defects. Common types of die errors include:

Die Cracks: Small fractures in the die that can transfer to the coin's surface.

Die Cuds: A portion of the die breaks off, leaving a raised area on the coin.

Doubled Die (DDO): A die is misaligned during production, resulting in doubled images or text on the coin.

Die Clash: When two dies come into contact without a planchet between them, transferring designs from one die to the other.

Planchet Errors:

Planchet errors occur when there's an issue with the metal disk, or planchet, that is used to strike the coin. These errors include:

Off-Center Strikes: When the planchet isn't aligned properly with the dies, causing part of the design to be missing.

Clipped Planchets: A planchet that is incorrectly cut, leading to a missing segment on the coin.

Wrong Planchet: A coin struck on a planchet intended for another denomination or metal composition.

Lamination Errors: When layers of metal on the planchet peel off, leaving a visible flaw on the coin's surface.

Striking Errors:

STRIKE ERRORS

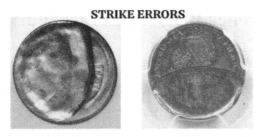

Striking errors occur during the actual coin striking process, where the planchet is fed into the press, and the design is stamped onto it. Some common striking errors include:

Weak Strikes: When the die fails to make full contact with the planchet, causing a faint or incomplete design.

Double Strikes: When a coin is struck more than once, either in the same location or off-center.

Brockages: When a coin is struck against another coin, leaving a mirrored, raised image of the design on the coin.

Multiple Strikes: When a coin receives multiple strikes in different positions, resulting in an overlapping design.

Difference Between Errors, Varieties, and Counterfeits

While errors, varieties, and counterfeits may seem similar, they are distinct terms within the numismatic world:

> **Errors**: As explained above, errors occur during the production process and are unintended anomalies on coins. These mistakes are rare and are generally seen as valuable by collectors due to their uniqueness and rarity.

> **Varieties**: A variety refers to a change in the design or characteristics of a coin that is intentionally made by the Mint, usually in response to a change in the coin's design or specifications. Varieties occur within a particular year or series of coins and are often considered legitimate differences. For example, a slight change in the position of a letter or number from one minting to another could create a variety. Unlike errors, varieties are usually produced on purpose and are not the result of a minting mistake.

Counterfeits: Counterfeits are imitation coins created to deceive collectors into thinking they are real. These coins are intentionally forged with the aim of tricking buyers into paying for them as if they were genuine error coins. Unlike errors, which occur naturally during minting, counterfeits are fraudulent creations designed to mimic the appearance of real coins.

CHAPTER TWO

Common Types of US Error Coins

Error coins are classified based on where and how the anomaly occurs during the minting process. These can be divided into several categories: die errors, planchet errors, striking errors, and other specific error types. Each category represents a different phase in the production of a coin, from the creation of the dies to the actual striking of the coin.

Die Errors

Die errors are caused by flaws or defects in the coin's die. The die is the tool used to strike the design into the planchet. Over time, dies can develop wear and cracks, or they might not align correctly during the minting process, leading to various types of die errors:

- **Misaligned   Dies**:
  This error occurs when the two dies (obverse
  and reverse) are not aligned properly when
  striking the coin. As a result, part of the coin's
  design may be off-center or completely
  missing. Misaligned die errors are relatively
  common and can range from slight
  misalignments to extreme cases where a
  significant portion of the design is out of
  alignment.

- **Double   Strikes**:
  A double strike happens when a coin is struck
  more than once by the same die, either in the
  same position or in a slightly shifted position.
  The result is a coin with overlapping designs.
  This error can occur when the coin is not
  ejected properly from the press after the first
  strike, allowing it to be struck again. Double
  strikes are often quite dramatic and can be an
  exciting find for collectors.

- **Overstrikes**:
  An overstrike occurs when a coin is struck on top of another coin, effectively "re-striking" the coin. The result is a coin that has two distinct designs, often with one being slightly visible beneath the other. Overstrikes can sometimes lead to coins being misidentified, as they can resemble certain types of die errors.

- **Die   Cracks**:
  Over time, the dies used to strike coins can develop cracks, and these cracks can transfer to the surface of the coin. A die crack is usually a thin line that appears on the coin's surface and may be visible in various areas, such as along the edge of the coin or through the design. Die cracks can also develop into more prominent features, such as die breaks or cuds.

Planchet Errors

Planchet errors occur when there is a problem with the planchet—the metal disk that is struck to produce the coin. These errors can happen if the planchet is improperly prepared or damaged before being struck. The types of planchet errors include:

- **Off-Center   Strikes**: Off-center strikes happen when the planchet is not properly aligned with the dies during the striking process. This results in a coin where the design is only partially visible or the image is shifted to one side. The more off-center the strike, the more dramatic and collectible the error becomes. In some extreme cases, the design may be completely missing from one side of the coin.

- **Clipped   Planchets**: A clipped planchet is a coin that has a section missing from its edge due to the planchet being improperly cut from the metal strip. These errors occur when the coin is struck with part of the planchet missing, resulting in a "clipped" appearance. Clipped planchets are highly prized by collectors, especially when the clip is noticeable and the coin remains identifiable.

- **Wrong Planchet Material**: On rare occasions, a coin may be struck on the wrong type of planchet. For example, a copper penny may be struck on a nickel planchet, or a coin intended for one denomination may be struck on a planchet meant for another. This results in a coin that is physically different from what was intended, often with significant differences in color, weight, and appearance.

Striking Errors

Striking errors occur during the actual coin-striking process. These errors happen when the press or the striking mechanism malfunctions, or when the coin is struck improperly. Common striking errors include:

- **Weak Strikes**: A weak strike occurs when the die fails to make full contact with the planchet, usually because of low pressure or a worn die. As a result, the coin's design may appear faint, incomplete, or poorly defined. Weak strikes are often found on older coins with worn dies but can also occur during the initial striking process.

- **Brockages**:
Brockages are striking errors that occur when a coin is struck against another coin, creating a mirrored, raised image of the coin's design on the obverse or reverse. This typically happens when a coin becomes lodged between the dies, causing the opposite side of the coin to strike the new planchet. Brockages can produce strikingly dramatic coins and are highly prized by collectors.

- **Multiple   Strikes**:
A multiple strike happens when a coin is struck more than once but in different positions. This results in a coin with overlapping or misaligned designs. Multiple strikes can often produce unique and visually

interesting error coins that are considered highly collectible.

Other Errors

In addition to the common die, planchet, and striking errors, there are a few other specific error types that are particularly famous or noteworthy:

- **Doubled Die Obverse (DDO)**: A doubled die obverse error occurs when the die is misaligned during the engraving process, resulting in the design being struck twice in different positions. This can cause doubling of the letters or numbers on the coin's obverse, making the design appear as though it is "shifted" or "doubled." One of the most famous examples of a doubled die is the 1955 Lincoln cent.

- **Doubled Die Reverse (DDR)**: A doubled die reverse is similar to a DDO but occurs on the reverse side of the coin. This error happens when the reverse die is misaligned or re-engravings occur during the die preparation process, causing the design to appear doubled. The 1972 Lincoln cent is a well-known example of this type of error.

- **Other Specific Error Types**: Other types of error coins include things like **broadstrikes** (coins that are struck outside the collar, causing them to spread beyond their normal borders), **gas bubbles** (from gas trapped in the metal), and **re-punched mintmarks** (where the mintmark is struck more than once).

CHAPTER THREE

Error Coin Identification

I dentifying error coins can be both a rewarding and challenging experience for collectors. While some errors are easy to spot, others may require a keen eye and a bit of practice. Understanding the common types of errors and knowing the right tools and resources for identification can greatly improve your ability to find and assess error coins in circulation.

How to Identify Common Errors in Circulation

When examining coins for errors, there are several key aspects to focus on. Many errors will be visible to the naked eye, while others may require closer inspection. Here are some tips for identifying common error types in circulation:

- **Look for Misalignments**: Misaligned die errors can often be seen with a simple inspection. If the design appears off-center or incomplete, this could indicate a misaligned die. The more extreme the misalignment, the easier it is to spot. For instance, a coin with a dic shift that results in a portion of the design missing is a clear indication of this type of error.

- **Examine for Double Strikes or Overstrikes**: Double strikes are one of the most obvious types of errors to identify. If you notice overlapping designs or text on a coin, or if part of the coin's design appears to be doubled, you could be looking at a double strike. Overstrikes are more subtle but can be identified by examining the coin for two different images or designs.

- **Check for Clipped Planchets**: Clipped planchets are easy to identify by looking for irregular edges. If you notice a coin with a section missing from the edge or a rounded, uneven outline, it may be a clipped planchet. These errors typically result from the planchet being cut incorrectly before being struck.

- **Inspect for Weak Strikes or Poor Detailing**: Weak strikes occur when the die does not make full contact with the planchet, leading to faint or incomplete designs. If a coin looks blurry or lacks sharp detail, it could be the result of a weak strike. Compare the coin to others of the same type to identify differences in sharpness and clarity.

- **Look for Brockages or Multiple Strikes**: Brockages often leave one side of the coin with a mirrored image of the other side's design. Multiple strikes can create overlapping or misaligned images. If you notice unusual overlapping designs or features that seem duplicated, these could be signs of a brockage or multiple strikes.

- **Check for Doubling**: Doubled dies are one of the most famous and collectible error types. When the text or design on a coin appears doubled (either slightly or more prominently), it's often a doubled die error. A close inspection of the text or design details, particularly on coins like the 1955 doubled die penny, can help you spot this error.

Tools and Resources for Identifying Error Coins

Identifying error coins requires a few basic tools, along with the right knowledge. Here are some essential tools and resources to help you identify and assess error coins:

- **Magnifying Tools**: A magnifying glass or loupe is essential for closely examining coins, especially when inspecting for fine details like doubled dies, die cracks, or weak strikes. A good quality magnifying loupe (preferably 10x magnification) will allow you to see the intricate details that are key to identifying errors.

- **Digital   Microscopes**: For more detailed inspections, digital microscopes can offer high magnification and the ability to capture clear images of coins. Some digital microscopes come with built-in cameras, allowing you to take pictures or videos for further analysis.

- **Reference   Guides**: Numismatic reference books are a valuable resource for identifying error coins. Guides like "The Complete Guide to Lincoln Cents" or "Strike It Rich With Pocket Change" provide detailed information and images of known error coins, helping collectors understand what to look for. These books also offer tips on identifying common and rare error coins.

- **Websites and Online Databases**: There are several websites dedicated to error coin identification. Popular sites like the **Error Coin Database** and **CoinHelp!** provide detailed descriptions and photos of error coins. Online communities and forums like **Collectors Universe** or **The Coin Community** are also great places to learn from other collectors and experts who can help you identify errors.

- **Coin Shows and Auctions**: Attending coin shows and auctions can be another valuable resource for identifying and learning about error coins. At these events, you can see examples of error coins firsthand, speak with experts, and sometimes purchase error coins from reputable dealers

.

- **Social Media and Collector Communities**: Social media platforms like Instagram and Facebook have vibrant coin-collecting communities. Following dedicated coin pages or joining groups focused on error coins can expose you to new discoveries and offer opportunities for advice and discussion.

Photos of Typical Errors for Visual Reference

Seeing errors firsthand is one of the best ways to recognize them. Below are a few examples of common errors and how they should appear on a coin:

- **Double Die (DDO/DDO)**

- **Clipped Planchet**

- **Off-Center Strike**

- **Brockage**:

- **Die Crack**:

CHAPTER FOUR

Rare and Valuable Error Coins

Error coins are often highly sought after by collectors due to their rarity and the uniqueness of the flaws they display. While most error coins are not worth a significant amount, there are some famous examples that have fetched substantial sums at auctions. In this section, we will highlight some of the most valuable and rare U.S. error coins, as well as the process of evaluating their value and where to find them in the marketplace.

Some of the Most Valuable and Rare US Error Coins

Several U.S. error coins have become legendary in the numismatic world due to their rarity, history, and value. Some of these coins have sold for millions of dollars at auction, making them prized possessions for collectors. Here are some of the most famous and valuable error coins:

- **1955 Doubled Die Lincoln Cent (DDO)**

One of the most well-known error coins in U.S. numismatics, the 1955 Doubled Die Lincoln Cent is famous for the visible doubling of the word "Liberty" and the date. The doubling occurred when the die was misaligned during engraving, resulting in the design being struck multiple times. While there were several thousand of these coins produced, most are in poor condition, making well-preserved examples very valuable. In 2008, one of these coins sold for over $300,000.

- **1943 Copper Penny**

During World War II, the U.S. Mint produced pennies made of steel in order to conserve copper for the war effort. However, a small number of copper planchets, which were intended for other coins, were accidentally used to strike 1943 pennies. This rare error resulted in a copper penny that is worth far more than its nominal value. A 1943 copper penny in good condition has sold for over $1 million, making it one of the most valuable error coins in history.

- **1913 Liberty Head Nickel**

The 1913 Liberty Head Nickel is perhaps one of the most famous error coins in U.S. history. Only five examples of this coin were ever produced, and they are all considered to be minting errors. The design was supposed to have been replaced by the Buffalo Nickel, but five coins were struck with the old Liberty Head design. These coins are worth millions of dollars, and they have become legendary in the world of numismatics. The highest price ever paid for one of these nickels was $4.5 million in 2018.

- **1972 Doubled Die Lincoln Cent (DDR)**

Another famous doubled die error is the 1972 Lincoln cent, which features a dramatic doubling of the word "Liberty" and the date. This error is particularly significant because the 1972 doubled die was widely known but not immediately understood by collectors, causing confusion at the time. Depending on the condition and degree of doubling, these coins can fetch anywhere from hundreds to thousands of dollars at auction.

- **2000 Sacagawea Dollar with Missing Edge Lettering**

A less common but still valuable error coin, the 2000 Sacagawea dollar with missing edge lettering is a sought-after collector's item. Normally, these coins feature edge lettering that reads "E PLURIBUS UNUM," but a few were struck without this feature. The error makes the coin stand out among other Sacagawea dollars, and some examples have sold for over $10,000 in well-preserved condition.

- **1937-D Three-Legged Buffalo Nickel**

The 1937-D Three-Legged Buffalo Nickel is a famous error coin in which one of the buffalo's legs was mistakenly polished off the die. This resulted in a coin with only three visible legs. While the error was caught early and many coins were destroyed, a few remain in circulation, making this coin highly desirable to collectors. In excellent condition, a 1937-D Three-Legged Buffalo Nickel can be worth tens of thousands of dollars.

The Process of Evaluating the Value of an Error Coin

The value of an error coin is influenced by several factors, which can make evaluating its worth a nuanced process. While rarity is a significant determinant, collectors also consider factors like condition, demand, and historical significance. Here are the key elements that influence an error coin's value:

Condition   (Grade):
The condition of a coin is one of the most important factors in determining its value. Coins are graded on a scale from 1 to 70, with 70 being perfect condition. Error coins that are well-preserved, with minimal wear and clear, visible errors, are far more valuable than those that are damaged or heavily worn. Professional grading services like the **Professional Coin Grading Service (PCGS)** or **Numismatic Guaranty Corporation (NGC)** provide a trusted certification of a coin's condition, which can significantly impact its market value.

- **Rarity**:
  The rarity of an error coin plays a crucial role in determining its value. Rare errors, such as the 1943 copper penny, are highly valuable due to their extreme scarcity. The number of

known examples of a particular error, along with the likelihood of finding another one, increases its value. Coins that are errors due to mistakes in production, or those that were made in limited numbers, are especially coveted by collectors.

- **Demand**:
The demand for error coins can fluctuate based on market trends, the popularity of a particular coin, and collector interest. Some error coins may become valuable simply because they are in high demand among numismatists and investors. Famous error coins, like the 1955 doubled die penny, maintain strong demand due to their iconic status in the numismatic community.

- **Historical   Significance**:
Coins with significant historical context or that are tied to key moments in U.S. history

often carry a higher value. The 1913 Liberty Head Nickel, for example, has not only a rare error but also a fascinating backstory that adds to its appeal. Error coins that represent important historical events, changes in minting practices, or even coin design transitions can command higher prices in the marketplace.

Auctions and Markets for Error Coins

Error coins are actively bought and sold in several key marketplaces, including auctions, online platforms, and physical coin shows. If you're looking to buy or sell error coins, here are some places to consider:

- **Coin   Auctions**: High-end error coins are often sold at specialized coin auctions, such as those held by companies like **Heritage Auctions**, **Stack's Bowers**, and **Sotheby's**. These auctions attract serious collectors and dealers who are willing to pay top dollar for rare error coins. Some coins have sold for millions at these auctions, making them an important venue for finding or selling high-value errors.

- **Online   Marketplaces**: Websites like **eBay** and **Heritage Auctions' online platform** are popular places to buy and sell error coins. However, buyers and sellers must exercise caution, as some listings may not be accurately described, and counterfeit coins can sometimes appear on the market. It's recommended to check the seller's feedback and get coins certified by a trusted grading service to ensure authenticity.

- **Coin   Shows**: Major coin shows like the **American Numismatic Association (ANA) World's Fair of Money** and regional coin conventions provide opportunities for collectors to interact with dealers, see error coins in person, and make purchases. Coin shows can be a great place to discover rare finds and network with other collectors and experts in the field.

Specialty Retailers and Dealers: Many coin dealers specialize in error coins and can be found through online searches or at local shops. These dealers often have direct access to error coins from both private collections and public sales, and they can provide valuable advice for collectors looking to purchase or sell error coins.

CHAPTER FIVE

Grading and Certification

G rading and certification are crucial components of the numismatic process, especially when it comes to error coins. The condition of an error coin and its authenticity play a significant role in determining its value. This section explores how error coins are graded, the importance of certification, and the role of major grading organizations in ensuring the accuracy and integrity of error coin assessments.

How Error Coins Are Graded

Grading is the process of evaluating a coin's condition and assigning it a grade based on various criteria. Coins are assessed on a scale of 1 to 70, with 70 being a perfect, flawless coin. When it comes to error coins, grading involves not only the usual condition factors but also an evaluation of the error itself. Here's an overview of how error coins are graded:

US ERROR COINS GUIDE 2025

- **Coin   Surface**:
The overall surface of the coin is inspected for wear, scratches, scuff marks, or any other damage. Coins with errors should be free from heavy abrasions, as these can detract from their value. Even though errors may make the coin visually distinct, they should not cause significant damage to the coin's overall surface.

- **The   Error**:
The type, size, and visibility of the error are all taken into account. For example, a well-defined double die or misaligned die error is more valuable than a subtle one that's hard to detect. The placement of the error (e.g., on the obverse or reverse), as well as how it impacts the design, also affects the grading.

- **Strike   Quality**:
A well-struck coin, even with an error, will

typically grade higher than a poorly struck one. If an error causes part of the design to be incomplete or faint, this can lower the grade. Brockages or die cracks, while valuable, may also affect the grading if they cause significant design distortion or other visual flaws.

- **Toning and Patina**: Toning, which is the natural color change that occurs over time, can either enhance or reduce the appeal of an error coin. A coin with a desirable patina and minimal damage may receive a higher grade. However, coins with unattractive or excessive toning may have a lower grade.

- **Luster**: Luster refers to the coin's shine and the way it reflects light. Coins with strong luster are considered more desirable, and this quality is especially important when grading error coins.

If an error occurs but the coin has lost much of its luster due to circulation, its grade will likely be lower.

Importance of Certification

Certification is the process of having an error coin evaluated and graded by a professional third-party service. Certification provides several benefits for collectors and sellers alike:

- **Authenticity   Verification**: Error coins, especially rare ones, are often targeted by counterfeiters. Having a coin certified by a reputable organization ensures that it is genuine and accurately described. Certification helps protect buyers from purchasing fake or misrepresented coins and gives sellers a way to prove their coin's authenticity.

- **Value   Preservation**: Certified coins are more likely to retain their value over time, as the certification process provides a level of trust and confidence to buyers and collectors. A coin's grade, as determined by a trusted third party, can help establish its market value. Uncertified error coins may be viewed with suspicion and have difficulty reaching their full potential value.

- **Marketability**:
  Certified error coins are much easier to sell, as buyers are more likely to trust the opinion of a professional grading service. Whether you are selling your coin to a dealer or at an auction, certification can significantly improve the coin's marketability and attractiveness to buyers.

- **Peace of Mind**:
  For collectors, owning a certified error coin provides peace of mind knowing that the coin has been thoroughly evaluated by experts. Certification helps eliminate uncertainty and ensures that the coin has been properly assessed in terms of its error and overall condition.

Where to Get Error Coins Certified

Several reputable grading organizations offer certification services for error coins. These organizations have strict standards and guidelines for evaluating and grading coins, and their certifications are widely recognized in the numismatic community. The two most prominent certification agencies for error coins are:

- **Professional Coin Grading Service (PCGS)** Founded in 1986, **PCGS** is one of the leading and most respected coin grading services in the world. PCGS is known for its high standards and its expertise in grading error coins. It provides a number of services, including coin certification, coin encapsulation, and a widely recognized grading scale. Many of the most valuable error coins, including rare examples like the 1955 Doubled Die Lincoln Cent, have been certified by PCGS.
  - **Services**: PCGS offers online verification of certification, and it also provides resources like population reports and historical price guides.

- o **How to Submit**: Coins can be submitted to PCGS through their website, or via one of their authorized dealers. They offer both regular and expedited services, depending on the value and urgency of the submission.

- **Numismatic Guaranty Corporation (NGC)** Established in 1987, **NGC** is another leading certification agency with a strong reputation for grading error coins. NGC is known for its rigorous grading process and its wide range of services for coin collectors, including grading, conservation, and certification.
  - o **Services**: NGC provides certified grading for error coins, along with additional services like conservation and imaging. NGC also maintains an extensive online database for coin certification verification and population reports.
  - o **How to Submit**: NGC accepts direct submissions through their website, or

through authorized dealers and coin shows.

- **Other Grading Services**: In addition to PCGS and NGC, other certification agencies like **ANACS** (American Numismatic Association Certification Service) and **ICG** (Independent Coin Graders) also offer grading services, though they may not have the same level of recognition or prestige as PCGS and NGC. It's important to choose a grading service that is widely accepted within the numismatic community to ensure the credibility and value of your coin.

The Role of Major Grading Organizations

Major grading organizations like PCGS and NGC play a pivotal role in the world of error coin collecting. Their certified grades set the standard for the value and authenticity of error coins, and their services provide transparency in the numismatic market. Here are some key ways these organizations influence the error coin market:

- **Establishing   Trust**: Professional grading organizations provide independent and unbiased assessments of coins, which helps establish trust between buyers and sellers. Coins that are graded and certified by these organizations are considered more reliable, leading to higher demand and market stability.

- **Market   Standards**: PCGS and NGC set the market standards for coin grading, and their grading criteria are widely adopted in the industry. Their expertise ensures that error coins are graded based on consistent, objective factors, which helps collectors make informed decisions.

- **Population Reports and Pricing Data**: Both PCGS and NGC offer valuable tools for collectors, such as population reports, which list the number of coins of a specific type or grade that have been certified. This helps collectors understand the rarity of error coins and their potential value in the marketplace. Additionally, both organizations offer historical pricing data, giving collectors insight into trends and potential investment opportunities.

- **Encapsulation and Protection**: Once an error coin is certified, it is encapsulated in a protective plastic holder, known as a **slab**, which prevents damage and ensures that the coin's condition is preserved for future generations. This encapsulation also includes a label that displays the coin's grade, certification number, and other relevant details, making it easy to verify the coin's authenticity.

CHAPTER SIX

Famous Error Coin Cases

Some error coins have made their way into the annals of numismatic history, becoming famous not only for their rarity but also for the fascinating stories behind their discovery, legal battles, and astronomical auction sales. These coins are often surrounded by tales of intrigue, mystery, and incredible fortune, and they serve as iconic symbols of the unpredictability and allure of coin collecting. In this section, we'll delve into some of the most famous error coin cases and the unique stories behind them.

The 1913 Liberty Head Nickel

Perhaps the most famous and coveted error coin in U.S. history, the **1913 Liberty Head Nickel** was produced in direct defiance of U.S. Mint policies. The Liberty Head design, which had been used since 1883, was officially replaced by the Buffalo Nickel in 1913. However, five coins bearing the Liberty

Head design were secretly struck by employees at the Mint, likely without the knowledge of Mint officials.

- **Discovery**:
  The 1913 Liberty Head Nickel remained unknown to the public until 1920 when a collector named **Samuel W. Brown** was able to purchase one of the five coins. Brown, a well-known collector of rare coins, managed to secure the nickel after it had been circulating for several years. Over time, he was able to locate and purchase the remaining four coins, making the 1913 Liberty Head Nickels one of the most sought-after pieces in numismatics.

- **Legal   Battle**:
The coins' status as "errors" created confusion, and over the years, questions about their authenticity and ownership surfaced. The U.S. Mint issued statements claiming that these coins were not officially produced, but their existence was undeniable. In 1967, one of the 1913 Liberty Head Nickels was stolen from a private collection, only to be recovered years later. In the years since, these coins have been sold for millions of dollars, with one coin fetching **$4.5 million** in 2018, setting a record for the most expensive U.S. coin ever sold at that time.

- **Legacy**:
The 1913 Liberty Head Nickel remains one of the most famous error coins ever discovered. Its fascinating history, as well as the mystery of its creation, has made it a legendary piece in the world of numismatics.

The 1943 Copper Penny

The **1943 Copper Penny** is another iconic error coin, notorious for its rarity and historical significance. During World War II, the U.S. Mint switched to producing steel pennies in order to conserve copper for military use. However, a small number of copper planchets—intended for other coins—were mistakenly used to strike 1943 pennies.

- **Discovery**:
  The discovery of the 1943 copper penny was initially met with skepticism, and many early examples were thought to be counterfeit. The first confirmed discovery occurred in 1947 when a coin collector found one in a roll of pennies. Over time, more of these rare copper

pennies were found, and they became one of the most valuable error coins in U.S. history.

- **Legal   Issues**: The U.S. Mint initially refused to acknowledge the existence of the copper pennies and discouraged people from attempting to sell them. In the 1940s and 1950s, some of these rare pennies were seized by the government, as it was feared that the coins were made from stolen copper planchets. Nonetheless, the existence of the coins was widely acknowledged, and they began to surface in private collections and auctions.

- **Auction   Sales**: The 1943 copper penny is one of the most valuable error coins ever produced, with examples regularly fetching high prices at auction. In 2012, a **1943 copper penny** was sold for more than **$1.7 million**, solidifying its place in numismatic history as one of the most valuable and sought-after error coins.

The 1955 Doubled Die Lincoln Cent

The **1955 Doubled Die Lincoln Cent (DDO)** is one of the most famous examples of a doubled die error in U.S. coinage. In this case, the die used to strike the coin was improperly aligned during the minting process, causing the design elements to be struck multiple times, resulting in a noticeable doubling of the word **"Liberty"** and the date on the obverse.

- **Discovery**:
  The error was initially noticed by collectors shortly after the coins were released into circulation. Early reports of the doubled die were met with skepticism, but the distinctive nature of the error quickly made the coin a collector's dream. The 1955 DDO is easily identifiable by the sharp doubling of the inscriptions, which makes it one of the most recognized error coins in the world.

- **Value**:
  The 1955 Doubled Die Lincoln Cent became one of the most sought-after coins for collectors, and well-preserved examples can fetch substantial sums. Coins in **good condition** have sold for **$300,000** or more at auction, while coins in lesser condition are still highly collectible and can command prices in the range of several thousand dollars.

- **Legacy**:
  This error coin continues to be one of the most

celebrated and iconic pieces in the world of numismatics. The 1955 DDO represents the fascination collectors have with error coins and their ability to stand out among thousands of other coins, making it a central piece in any collection of error coins.

The 1972 Doubled Die Lincoln Cent

The **1972 Doubled Die Lincoln Cent (DDR)** is another well-known error coin featuring a dramatic doubling of the design elements, particularly the word **"Liberty"** and the date. The error was the result of an improper alignment of the die during the minting process, which caused multiple strikes of the same design.

- **Discovery**:
  The 1972 DDR was noticed soon after the

coins were released into circulation, but its true significance took some time to be fully appreciated. Many of the early examples were overlooked or mistaken for wear, but more collectors soon recognized the distinctive doubling that made these coins valuable. Today, the 1972 DDR remains one of the most popular error coins among collectors.

- **Value**:
  The value of the 1972 Doubled Die Lincoln Cent can range greatly depending on the severity of the doubling and the condition of the coin. Well-preserved examples can sell for **several thousand dollars**, while coins in lesser condition still retain considerable value. In particularly good condition, the 1972 DDR can fetch upwards of **$20,000**.

Other Notable Error Coin Cases

- **The 2000 Sacagawea Dollar with Missing Edge   Lettering**
  A small number of 2000 Sacagawea dollars

were struck without the usual edge lettering that reads "E PLURIBUS UNUM." These coins are extremely rare and valuable, with some selling for over **$10,000** at auction. The error was a result of a mistake during the minting process, and it was quickly discovered, making these error coins a unique and highly sought-after collectible.

- **The 1937-D Three-Legged Buffalo Nickel**
  The 1937-D Three-Legged Buffalo Nickel is another iconic error coin. The mistake occurred when one of the buffalo's legs was accidentally removed during the minting process. Only a small number of these coins were struck before the error was noticed, and they remain highly valuable today, with coins in good condition fetching tens of thousands of dollars.

These famous error coin cases not only highlight the rarity and value of certain coins but also demonstrate how error coins can sometimes take on a life of their own, becoming legendary pieces of numismatic history. The stories behind these coins add an element of intrigue and excitement to the world of coin collecting, making error coins an enduring fascination for collectors and investors alike.

CHAPTER SEVEN

The Future of US Error Coins

The world of error coins is constantly evolving, driven by changes in minting technology, production processes, and the growing demand from collectors. As the U.S. Mint continues to innovate and refine its manufacturing methods, error coins may become both rarer and more fascinating. In this section, we explore the future of U.S. error coins, examining how advancements in technology, improvements in minting processes, and shifting numismatic trends might shape the future of error production and their value.

Evolving Minting Processes and the Impact on Error Coin Production

As the U.S. Mint embraces technological advancements and refines its production techniques, the occurrence of error coins may decrease.

Historically, error coins were often the result of imperfections in the minting process—such as worn or misaligned dies, defective planchets, and issues with the machinery. However, with the ongoing refinement of the Mint's processes, many of these common sources of error are being mitigated.

- **Precision in Modern Minting**: The U.S. Mint has increasingly adopted modern technology that prioritizes precision in every stage of the coin production process. Automated systems, precise die alignment machines, and better quality control have all contributed to reducing the occurrence of errors. Modern minting techniques allow for faster production times and more consistent results, which significantly reduces the likelihood of producing error coins.

- **Automation and Error Reduction**: Automation has allowed for better calibration of dies and machinery, minimizing the human errors that often led to mistakes in earlier coinage. For example, the integration of robotic systems into the minting process helps ensure that coins are properly struck and aligned, reducing the frequency of misalignments, double strikes, and other die-related errors.

While these advances in technology are undoubtedly beneficial for ensuring high-quality production, they also mean that the chances of error coins—particularly the more obvious ones—will continue to decrease. However, error coins will not disappear entirely; instead, they may become more unique, often arising from more complex or technical causes.

Technological Advances and Their Impact on Error Coin Production

The introduction of cutting-edge technology, such as **laser etching** and **advanced die engraving**, is also reshaping the way coins are produced. These technologies allow for greater detail, more intricate designs, and improved coin durability. While these innovations improve the quality of the coinage, they also present new opportunities for error coins to emerge—albeit in more subtle or intricate ways.

- **Laser Etching and Die Engraving**: Laser etching, used for creating intricate designs and microscopic details, could lead to new types of error coins. Errors in laser engraving, such as unintended designs, misaligned etchings, or "ghosting" (when a faint second engraving overlaps the original), could produce error coins that are harder to identify but nonetheless valuable.

  Similarly, advancements in die engraving might introduce errors tied to the precision of machine settings, which could cause issues like unintended distortions or the appearance of irregularities in the die itself. As these new methods gain popularity, more nuanced error types could emerge, further complicating the traditional process of identification.

- **Machine Improvements and Error Types**: As machinery continues to improve, the possibility of errors will shift from simple misalignments to more complex, technical issues. For instance, a machine malfunction might lead to defects in the metal planchet or create an unusual surface finish, resulting in more distinctive error coins. These kinds of errors may be rarer but will likely be even more intriguing to collectors due to their novelty.

While technological advancements will lead to fewer traditional types of errors (like double strikes or off-center coins), they may pave the way for new, rarer types of errors that collectors will eagerly seek out.

Predictions for the Future Value and Types of Error Coins

With the evolving minting processes and the impact of modern technology, the future of U.S. error coins will likely see a shift in both the types of errors produced and the value attributed to them. As fewer coins are struck with obvious errors, the demand for rare and unique error coins will likely rise. Here are some predictions about the future of U.S. error coins:

- **Rarer Error Types**: As the common sources of error (like die misalignment or planchet defects) become less frequent, more sophisticated errors—perhaps stemming from new technology—may become the focus of collectors. These types of errors may be more difficult to identify and will likely require a greater level of expertise to recognize. These coins will be rare, and their uniqueness will drive up demand and value. For example, a mistake involving new technologies, such as engraving errors created by the miscalibration of laser etching machines, could lead to exciting and valuable discoveries.

- **Higher Value for Exceptional Errors**: As error coins become less common, the value of exceptional, rare examples will likely increase. Coins with complex errors, like those that are the result of advanced technological mishaps, could fetch even higher prices at auctions. Collectors will continue to seek out coins with striking and dramatic errors, especially those that are truly one-of-a-kind or have a compelling backstory of discovery.

  For example, a coin featuring an unusual error, such as a combination of two different errors (a double die with an off-center strike), could command a higher value than any error of its individual components. As rare and unique error coins become harder to find, collectors will be more willing to pay a premium for these rarities.

- **Increased Demand from Collectors**: The rarity and increasing awareness of error coins will lead to greater interest and demand from both seasoned collectors and new enthusiasts. As more collectors become aware of the allure of error coins and the potential for higher returns on investment, the market for these coins will continue to grow. Additionally, as collectors seek out error coins with historical significance or unique features, more individuals may be inclined to purchase them, further driving up prices.

- **Technological Changes in Authentication**: As technology improves, so will the tools for identifying and authenticating error coins. The development of AI and machine learning could enhance the process of detecting errors in coins, making it easier for numismatists and collectors to identify rare errors with greater precision. These advancements could lead to more rigorous authentication, ensuring that only authentic error coins are sold and circulated within the marketplace, further increasing the reliability and value of error coins.

Conclusion: The Ever-Changing World of Error Coins

While the future of U.S. error coins may be shaped by new technologies and improved minting practices, one thing is certain: error coins will always be a fascinating part of numismatic history. As technology progresses and the minting process becomes more refined, error coins may become rarer and more complex. For collectors, this will only enhance the allure and value of the remaining errors, making them even more precious and desirable.

The ever-evolving world of U.S. error coins will continue to captivate numismatists and coin enthusiasts alike, ensuring that these remarkable pieces of history remain a central focus of the coin-collecting world for generations to come

CHAPTER EIGHT

How to Buy and Sell Error Coins

Navigating the world of buying and selling error coins can be both exciting and challenging. The rarity and value of these coins make them highly sought after, but they also come with risks, especially when it comes to authenticity. This section provides valuable tips for buying and selling error coins, helping you ensure that your transactions are legitimate and that you make informed decisions in the marketplace.

Tips for Buying Error Coins from Reputable Dealers or Auctions

When buying error coins, it's essential to work with reputable dealers and auction houses to avoid pitfalls. The market for error coins is filled with counterfeit coins, misrepresented pieces, and less-than-reputable sellers. To ensure a smooth transaction and to acquire authentic error coins, follow these tips:

- **Research Trusted Dealers**: Start by researching well-known and trusted dealers who specialize in error coins and numismatics. Established dealers often have a track record of selling authentic error coins and can provide you with detailed information on the pieces they are offering. Look for dealers who are members of recognized numismatic organizations, such as the **American Numismatic Association (ANA)** or the **Professional Numismatists Guild (PNG),** as membership in these organizations is often a sign of trustworthiness.

- **Check for Certification**: Always buy error coins that have been certified by a reputable grading service. Coins graded by **PCGS (Professional Coin Grading Service)**, **NGC (Numismatic Guaranty Corporation)**, or **ANACS (American Numismatic Association**

Certification Service) have been authenticated and graded by experts. Certified error coins come with a guarantee of authenticity, which adds to their value and ensures that you're getting the real deal.

- **Attend Auctions and Coin Shows**: Auction houses like **Heritage Auctions**, **Stack's Bowers Galleries**, and **GreatCollections** are reputable sources for buying error coins. These auctions often feature rare and valuable error coins, many of which have been carefully examined and authenticated. Coin shows are also great places to meet dealers in person, see coins up close, and network with other collectors. Before attending, research the auction house or show's reputation to ensure you're dealing with an established and trustworthy source.

- **Ask for Provenance**: If possible, ask the seller for provenance (the coin's history of ownership). This can help confirm its authenticity and provide additional value. Provenance documentation can be particularly important for rare or high-value error coins, as it demonstrates the coin's legitimacy and its place in numismatic history.

- **Verify the Coin's Authenticity**: If you're unsure about a coin's authenticity, consider using a third-party authentication service before making a purchase. This is particularly important for high-value error coins. Many certification companies offer services for individual coins, where they verify the coin's authenticity and provide a detailed report.

Warning Signs of Fake or Misrepresented Error Coins

Unfortunately, the market for error coins also attracts counterfeiters and sellers who misrepresent their coins. Being able to spot a fake or misrepresented error coin can save you from costly mistakes. Here are some warning signs to watch out for:

- **Inconsistent or Poor-Quality Design**: Genuine error coins usually have clear and sharp features, even if the error itself is unusual. If the design seems blurry, inconsistent, or poorly struck, the coin may be a fake or poorly made replica. Pay close attention to the details in the design—counterfeiters often fail to replicate the fine intricacies of genuine coins.

- **Incorrect Weight or Size**: Error coins, while produced with irregularities, will generally retain the correct weight and size for their type. If an error coin feels unusually light or heavy, it could be a sign that the coin is counterfeit. A reputable dealer will always provide detailed specifications, and if the coin doesn't match the expected weight or diameter, it may be a fake.

- **Unnatural Patina or Wear**: Genuine error coins will typically have a patina that matches their age and the wear they've experienced in circulation. If the coin looks too shiny or its wear patterns appear unnatural, it could be a sign of a fake. Counterfeit coins often have a "fresh" appearance because they haven't gone through years of circulation or natural aging.

- **Suspicious   Prices**: If a deal sounds too good to be true, it probably is. Be cautious when buying error coins at significantly lower prices than the going market rate. While some error coins may be undervalued in certain circumstances, coins that are being sold at a fraction of their actual worth could be counterfeit or misrepresented. Always research the market value of the coin before making a purchase.

- **Lack of Documentation or Certification**: If the seller cannot provide certification or provenance, or if they are unwilling to let you verify the coin's authenticity, it's a major red flag. Be wary of private sellers who claim they don't need certification for an error coin. Trustworthy dealers will always provide some form of proof of authenticity.

Selling Your Error Coins

If you have error coins that you wish to sell, there are several ways to approach the process, and it's essential to understand the current market trends to maximize the value of your collection. Here are some tips for selling error coins:

- **Get Your Coins Certified**: Before selling your error coins, consider getting them certified by a reputable grading service like PCGS or NGC. Certification adds credibility to the coin and can increase its value by assuring potential buyers of its authenticity and quality. Certified coins are often easier to sell at a higher price.

- **Choose the Right Marketplace**: When selling error coins, you have several options, including online marketplaces, auctions, or direct sales to dealers. If you're looking for the best price, online auction houses like **Heritage Auctions** and **GreatCollections** can help you reach a global audience of collectors. Coin shows are also a great option for selling your coins in person, allowing you to negotiate directly with potential buyers.

- **Know the Market Trends**: Error coins are often affected by market trends, so it's important to stay informed about the current demand for specific types of error coins. Monitor auction results, follow numismatic publications, and track online marketplaces to get a sense of which coins are in demand. This will help you time your sale and ensure you get the best possible price.

- **Work with Reputable Dealers**: If you choose to sell your error coins through a dealer, make sure you're working with a trusted and reputable numismatic professional. Research the dealer's reputation and ask for references or reviews from other customers. Dealers will often offer to buy your coins directly, but their price may not be as high as what you would get through an auction or direct sale.

- **Don't   Rush   the   Sale**: Take your time when selling error coins, especially if they are rare or highly valuable. Rushing the sale could lead to getting less than your coins are worth. Be patient and wait for the right buyer or marketplace to ensure that you receive the best price.

Understanding Market Trends

The market for error coins is constantly fluctuating, and the value of specific coins can vary based on factors such as rarity, demand, and market conditions. Some error coins, like the **1955 Doubled Die Lincoln Cent**, have remained highly valuable for decades, while others may experience periods of heightened interest or decline.

To stay ahead of market trends, follow numismatic auctions, join online forums and communities of collectors, and subscribe to publications that focus on error coins. By staying informed, you'll be able to make smarter decisions when buying or selling error coins and ensure that you're making the most of your investments.

By following these tips for buying and selling error coins, you can confidently navigate the market, avoid common pitfalls, and maximize the value of your collection. Whether you're buying error coins to expand your collection or selling coins to capitalize on their value, understanding the nuances of the market and working with reputable sources is essential to ensuring a successful transaction.

CONCLUSION

Error coins have long captivated collectors, historians, and numismatists alike, standing as unique relics of the United States Mint's production process. These coins, often produced by mistake, carry with them a story of human error, technological limitations, and the fascinating unpredictability of minting. As we've explored throughout this guide, error coins hold great importance in U.S. numismatics, both for their rarity and for the insights they provide into the minting process itself.

Whether you're a seasoned collector or someone just starting to explore the world of error coins, this field offers a wealth of knowledge and excitement. From understanding the different types of errors to recognizing the rarest and most valuable specimens, there is always more to learn. Collectors who are diligent in their research and take the time to study the intricacies of error coins are sure to find both personal satisfaction and, potentially, significant financial rewards.

As technology continues to advance, and minting processes become increasingly precise, the production of error coins may become even more rare, making these exceptional pieces even more valuable and desirable. The future of error coin collecting is full of possibilities, and collectors are encouraged to stay curious, continue researching, and explore the fascinating world of error coins.

Ultimately, error coins are not just mistakes in metal—they are treasures that preserve a moment in time, showcasing the delicate balance between human hands and machinery. For those passionate about numismatics, error coins offer a tangible connection to history, offering a lasting legacy of the artistry and craftsmanship that defines U.S. coinage.

As you continue your journey into the world of error coins, remember that each coin tells its own story. Keep learning, keep exploring, and let your collection evolve with each unique discovery.

Made in United States
Orlando, FL
26 May 2025

61599447R00049